MARATHON RUNNING

A Beginners' Guide on Preparing to Run Your First Marathon

Matt Jordan

Table of Contents

What Is A Marathon?

When the climber George Mallory was asked why he wanted to summit Everest, he famously replied "Because it's there." The same words could be said by many a marathon runner. Of course, training for a marathon will make you fitter and stronger, but most seasoned racers compete time and again for the challenge, and the sheer thrill of finishing; because it's there.

This world-famous race of 26 miles and 385 yards had become the benchmark that all long-distance runners measure themselves against. It can be a social activity or a solo one, you can compete against other runners or you can try to beat your own best time. But it's a goal to aim for, something to strive towards, a challenge to set yourself. It's a huge accomplishment, and it's something only a small proportion of the population ever manages to complete.

This book will guide you through everything you need to run your first marathon. You will learn how to choose the right equipment, what to eat to keep your body in the best shape, the best exercises to do to make you stronger and more flexible, how to stay injury-free when you run, how to choose your marathon and what to do on the day. There's also a six-month training schedule that will gradually build up the miles, work on your strength and speed and push your endurance abilities, slowly but surely transforming you from complete novice to long-distance runner.

Are you ready to challenge yourself and test your limits? Let's get started!

A Brief History of Marathons

At the start of the 5th century BC, in the town of Marathon in Greece, a battle took place between the Athenians and the Persians. In spite of being hopelessly outnumbered, the Athenians defeated the invading Persian army.

Legend has it that Pheidippides, who was reputed to be the fastest runner in the Athenian army, was then asked to make the 26-mile run from Marathon to Athens to deliver news of the victory. He ran the whole distance without stopping and collapsed into the Assembly shouting "We have won!"

When the Olympic Games were revived at the end of the 19th century, the organisers wanted a popular event that would reflect the heroic origins of the ancient Greek Olympics. The legend of the marathon seemed ideal, and at the 1896 Olympic Games the first competitive marathon was run from Marathon to Athens. The distance was 25 miles, and it was won by Spyridon Louis in a time of 2 hours, 58 minutes and 50 seconds.

Louis was a Greek water-carrier who had never done any competitive running before. He started towards the back, but as more and more runners dropped out he took the lead. When word spread to the stadium that a Greek was leading, the crowd erupted into cheers and by the time Louis reached the stadium two Greek princes were there to accompany him on his final lap. The King of Greece told him he could name his prize, and Louis asked for a cart and donkey to help him in his business.

The first marathons were around 24 to 26 miles, roughly the distance between Marathon and Athens. The first race to be run at the incredibly specific distance of 26 miles and 385 yards was during the 1908 London Olympics. It was extended from the initial 26 miles so that the race would finish in front of the royal box inside the stadium, so that the royal family could observe.

As the race neared its end, the first person into the stadium was Italian runner Dorando Pietri, who had overtaken the leader Charles Hefferon at the 24th mile. He was so tired that he started running the wrong way around the track and had to be turned around by race officials. Now completely exhausted he collapsed several times as he finished his final lap, and all the while the other contestants were catching up. Finally the clerk and chief medical officer helped him pick himself up, and he still crossed the finish line a full 30 seconds in front of the runner-up.

That would not be the end of the matter. Some of the other participants complained that Pietri received help from officials against the rules, and he was disqualified and the trophy handed to Johnny Hayes of the USA. It was the most controversial event of the Olympics, and the excitement and drama had people talking about it for weeks and cemented the marathon's reputation; as well as ensuring 26.2 miles would become the standard distance.

After those great races, the marathon became a regular Olympic event and races were organised in cities around the world, although the initial competitions were only open to male participants. The IAAF considers Violet Piercy the first woman to set a world best in the marathon, when she ran in the Polytechnic Marathon in London in 1926, despite not having permission or a role as an official participant.

However, it wasn't until 1967 that a woman managed to run with a race number. Kathrine Switzer registered for the Boston Marathon as 'K.V. Switzer' and officials didn't realise she was a woman until she turned up to compete. There were objections, and race manager Jock Semple even tried to rip off Switzer's race number, which almost led to a punch up between him and Switzer's boyfriend. But finally she was allowed to race, and her finish made headlines around the world.

Things started to change after that, and in 1972 women were welcome in the Boston Marathon. By the 1984 Olympics in Los Angeles it had been decided that a women's marathon would be held in addition to the men's, the first official female winner of the Olympic marathon was Joan Benoit of the USA, who finished in 2 hours 24 minutes and 52 seconds.

The men's world record is currently held by Dennis Kimetto of Kenya, who ran the Berlin Marathon in 2014 in astonishing 2 hours 2 minutes and 57 seconds. The women's world record is held by Paula Radcliffe of Great Britain, who completed the London Marathon in 2003 in an equally impressive 2 hours 15 minutes and 25 seconds.

If you're worried that you're too old to start running marathons, take heart – the world's oldest marathon runner is Fauja Singh, who completed the Toronto Waterfront Marathon in 2011 at the age of 100. Singh didn't even start running until he was 81, when he immigrated to England to live with one of his sons after the death of his wife. He turned up to his first training session in a three-piece suit, but learned quickly and has gone on to run the Hong Kong, New York and London Marathons.

Most of the larger modern marathons are members of the Association of International Marathons and Distance Races (AIMS), which now has more than 400 different distance events in over 100 different countries. The largest of these, part of the World Marathon Majors, are the Berlin, Boston, Chicago, London, New York and Tokyo Marathons. If you run two or more of these races in a single year you are eligible for the WMM prize of $500,000, which goes to the male and female athlete who score the greatest number of points from any two qualifying races.

And if those six major races give you a taste, there are plenty of marathons run in some weird and wonderful places across the planet. The Tromsø Midnight Sun Marathon is run in Norway every June. The town of Tromsø is within the Arctic Circle and gets 24 hours of light in the middle of summer, so the race begins at 8.30pm so that participants can run in the 'midnight sun'. Even further north, the annual North Pole Marathon involves ten laps around a small loop of ice and snow, run in full winter gear in extremely variable weather conditions.

You can also choose to race in the Everest Marathon, but beware – it's a 15 day hike to base camp before you even think about running, and then a 15 day hike home. The world's highest marathon takes some acclimatising to the altitude and thin air, and the hills are steep, but the views can't be beaten. The views are also pretty spectacular on the Great Wall of China Marathon, although the steep and treacherous ascents and descents are not for the faint of heart.

One of the stranger marathons – originally a bet between two friends in a pub – is Llanwrtyd Wells' Man vs Horse Marathon. Although horses are obviously much faster, the mountainous and boggy terrain slows them down and gives the runners a sporting chance. Still, since the race began in 1980 only two men have ever beaten the horses.

The Athens Classic Marathon is staged in modern times along the original route taken by Pheidippides, and is considered one of the toughest marathons in the world with a brutal uphill climb between 10km and 31km. It passes through hilly terrain and goes past the tomb of the Athenian soldiers who fell in the battle 2,500 years ago before finishing in the Panathenaic Stadium, which has been the site of various athletic events since the 6th century BC. The marathon has spread around the world and come full circle, still being run in the place where it all started.

Correct Clothing and Footwear

By far the most important piece of kit for a runner is the shoes. Get this right and nothing else you wear matters that much – get it wrong and you're letting yourself in for a world of pain. The best shoe depends entirely on your feet, stance and running style, so make sure to choose a pair of shoes that suit you.

Your Running Style

When you run, you usually land towards the outside of your foot and then roll inward slightly until your foot is flat before you push off for the next step. That slight roll is called pronation, and it helps absorb the impact as you run. Some people have a large degree of pronation, which means they're rolling too far inward instead of staying straight, and eventually this can lead to injury.

How can you tell if you're pronating or not? If you're already a runner, you can look at the wear pattern on the bottom of your shoes. A lot of wear towards the inside of the shoe indicates that you over-pronate, while excessive wear on the outside might indicate you under-pronate. People with low arches tend to over-pronate and people with high arches tend to under-pronate.

You can also film yourself running – pretty easy to do on your smartphone and you only need ten seconds or so of footage to see how you run. Ask someone at the gym to film you briefly on the treadmill.

People who over-pronate need a shoe with motion control which will stabilise them as they run. People who under-pronate often don't have enough natural impact absorption, so they need a shoe with a lot of cushioning to prevent injury.

Cushioning

The trade-off with extra cushioning is that it always means extra weight. Well-cushioned shoes reduce the impact on your body and are more comfortable to wear, but light shoes allow you to run faster without feeling weighed down.

Beginners should start with a shoe with a decent amount of cushioning while they build up muscle and let their feet harden. Once you've been running for several months, if you have a good technique and neutral running style, lighter shoes may suit you better.

Some people swear by minimalist running shoes to avoid injury. The theory is that running in heavily-cushioned shoes encourages you to strike the heel of your foot hard against the ground, whereas when you run barefoot you land on your mid-foot and distribute the impact better. Minimalist shoes are designed to protect your feet from sharp objects but allow you to run as though you were barefoot. Barefoot running requires a specific technique, so it's best left to the more experienced. Get started in normal trainers and then you can always make the transition later on if you choose.

Purpose

If you already have cross-trainers that you use in the gym or for sports, don't be tempted to wear them to run in too. Cross-trainers are generally heavier than running shoes with more support for the lateral movements necessary in sport, but they will weigh you down on long runs.

The surface you intend to run on also affects the kind of shoe you should choose. Unfortunately, most of us have no choice but to run on the road, and harder surfaces have more impact on your joints and need more cushioning to compensate.

If your race is off-road and you intend to also train on rough ground, you will need a trail running shoe. Trail running shoes are wider with tougher soles, designed to provide support on uneven surfaces and defend your feet from sharp objects. They have more ankle support and protection, given how much more work your ankles do over rough terrain. The soles also have a lot more grip, which is unnecessary on roads but vital when running on wet grass or slippery rocks. Trail running shoes also have more durable uppers made of ripstop nylon to guard against tears from rocks or undergrowth.

Some runners like to wear a lighter shoe with less cushioning on race day, sometimes known as a 'performance' shoe. Carrying less weight on your feet can shave a few seconds per mile off your time, which for some people makes all the difference to their goal time. They don't have enough cushioning to run in every day, which is why you shouldn't train in one, and you should avoid them altogether if you under-pronate or have a tendency towards stress injuries.

Fit

Your feet swell when they get hot or during activity, so a pair of shoes that seem to fit in the shop may actually be too small. Your foot also spreads when you strike the ground, which means you want shoes that have a bit of extra room so they don't inhibit the natural motion of your foot. Most running shoes have a range of width fittings available in each size, to get a perfect fit for your shoe.

Running shoes come with different amounts of 'drop' - the difference between the height of the heel and the height of the toe. Most people feel more comfortable in shoes with a drop of around 8-12mm, but some people prefer a flatter shoe.

The jury is still out on whether shoes with less drop help prevent injury or not, so in general you should go with something that feels comfortable to you. If you're having trouble with heel-related injuries like plantar fasciitis or Achilles pain a bigger drop might help; alternatively, if you're having toe problems or pain at the front of your foot a lower drop will take some of the pressure off.

You should replace your shoes roughly every 500 miles. Old shoes do not cushion your feet as well as new ones, and the shoe upper can stretch out of shape slightly. Don't risk injury by running in worn-out shoes.

Clothing

If you've got a decent pair of running shoes, the rest of what you wear doesn't matter a great deal so long as it's loose and comfortable to exercise in. The exception to this is socks, which are almost as important as shoes for keeping your feet healthy.

Your feet will sweat as you run and wet socks lead to blisters, so you need a fabric that is breathable and wicks moisture. Smart fabrics like CoolMax or Dri-Fit will absorb sweat and keep it away from your skin, while cotton is one of the worst fabrics as it holds moisture and makes your feet damp. Wool is also a good fabric that absorbs a lot of moisture and keeps your feet warm in cold conditions, although it's not always as durable as man-made fabrics. Look out for socks with extra cushioning on the heel and toe if your feet get sore easily.

If you do want to buy dedicated running clothing, again go for technical clothing that wicks away sweat to keep you cool. Even in winter you need to keep moisture away from your skin because if it cools it can make you too cold.

Technical fabrics are also lighter than conventional cotton t-shirts, and every ounce helps when you're running long distances. Running clothing also has flat seams which prevent the fabric from chafing as you move, and bright colours and reflective strips mean you can be seen by traffic if you run when it's dark or in poor visibility.

In the last few years there's been more of an interest in compression wear for runners. Compression wear supposedly helps your circulation, and therefore clears lactic acid out of the muscles faster. It also decreases muscle oscillation, which reduces the force of impact on your body. Scientific studies suggest that while they do help, in most cases the benefits are minimal, and they certainly won't make you run any faster.

Naturally, you will warm up while you run, so dress for a temperature around 5 degrees warmer than the actual outside temperature. If it's cold enough to need a jacket then the soft-shell kind is breathable and won't hold moisture in and make you damp. You might want to wear a hat and gloves even if you're too warm for a jacket, since your extremities are exposed to the cold wind when you run and your hands and head can feel cold even if your core is warm.

For women a sports bra is a necessity – it's not at all comfortable to run without one, and you can injure the breast tissue without proper support. Sports bras come in low, medium and high impact options, and running is a high impact sport that needs the toughest bras available. Choose an encapsulating sports bra that has individual cups but also compresses the chest for the highest level of support, and check that it has reinforcing panels around the sides and underneath. Try the bra on and then jump up and down in the changing rooms; ideally nothing should move and the bra should feel snug but not so tight that you can't take a deep breath.

Other Accessories

If you're interval training (alternating walking and running or a gentle run with a hard one) then you need a watch to time your sessions. For that basic function any stopwatch will do, but a dedicated running watch will also collect a lot of vital statistics to improve your run. GPS capability means you don't have to work out how many miles you've run on a map, and the heart rate monitor lets you see if you're working as hard as you need to be. Some watches even measure your cadence and suggest areas for improvement, or have online programs that can analyse your performance and produce a personalised training plan.

Your smartphone can do many of these things with free or paid apps, but not everyone wants to take their phone running with them and it's easier to look at your watch than pull out your phone every couple of minutes.

Fitness trackers can also do some of these things but are mostly designed to track how many steps you take in a day and how well you sleep, and won't be as useful as a dedicated running watch.

Being outside much more means protecting yourself from the elements, even on sunny days. Wear sunglasses with UVA and UVB protection the kind that wrap around will stay on pretty well even when you're bouncing around, or you can get an elastic strap to hold them securely to your head. A hat also does a good job shielding your face from the sun, or if it makes you too hot then a visor will do the same job but let the air reach your head, and remember to always wear a high factor sunscreen to protect your skin.

For short runs you won't need water so long as you stay hydrated during the day and replace your fluids at the end of a run. For anything approaching an hour or more you want to carry water with you, as dehydration affects performance and can make you ill. You can either carry a hand-held one (they often have straps and ergonomic designs to make them easier to hold), or wear a waist belt with attachments for bottles. For longer runs you might want a light running backpack that has room for snacks and a first-aid kit. What kind of snacks you should take and what you should eat in general are covered in the next chapter.

Nutrition

It's important to fuel your body in a way that builds strength and stamina if you're going to finish the full 26.2 miles, especially if you're aiming for a fast time. Eating the right foods will make your runs feel easier and help you train better.

The more activity you do, the more calories you burn and the more you need to eat, but it might not be as much as you think. The average runner burns around 100 calories per mile, depending on weight and the efficiency of your running. That's the number of calories in a medium-size banana.

For short runs you only need a few extra snacks to sustain you, and if you're trying to lose weight then it's better to stick to roughly your normal number of calories. As you train harder your base metabolism will go up, and longer runs will mean you need to eat more. Weigh yourself regularly to make sure you're eating enough to maintain your weight, or if you are trying to lose weight then aim for no more than a pound per week to stay in the safe range.

Carbohydrates

You want around two-thirds of your daily calories to come from carbohydrates. Carbohydrates are the fuel that your body uses to produce energy. It's easier for your body to burn than fat, and at moderate or high levels of exercise it is your main source of ATP (adenosine triphosphate, a kind of 'unit of currency' of energy).

In order to make energy, your body first breaks the carbohydrate down into glucose. Whether you eat a baked potato, a sandwich or a chocolate bar, the carbohydrates (and sugar is a carbohydrate) will eventually be converted into glucose. So if they all end up the same, why is a baked potato healthier than a chocolate bar?

The more complex a carbohydrate is, the longer it takes your body to digest it. When you eat a complex carbohydrate, your body releases the energy gradually and you maintain a steady level of blood glucose. When you eat a simple sugar, your blood glucose goes up quickly but then quickly falls again as your body finishes digesting the sugar.

Simple carbohydrates aren't all bad – the sugar in your energy drink gets glucose to the muscles quickly, providing fuel if you're running or helping the recovery process if you've just finished. But for a long run like a marathon you want your body to keep releasing energy for as long as possible.

If you want to know whether a food is mostly simple or complex carbohydrates, you can check its Glycaemic Index (GI) or Glycaemic Load (GL). The GI shows how quickly the sugar will reach your blood, while the GL takes account of average serving sizes. A low GL food will help to keep your blood sugar more stable.

Don't forget that the GI and GL aren't absolute measures of how healthy something is – you need to also take into account the levels of fat, salt, vitamins and minerals. Not surprisingly, the complex carbohydrates favoured by most nutritionists are things like whole grain bread, whole wheat pasta and brown rice, which also contain fibre and additional necessary nutrients, which processed foods do not have.

Protein

Your body doesn't use protein as fuel, but to repair and strengthen itself, especially the muscles and tendons. It's also necessary for a whole host of other activities like hormone production, cell repair and fluid balance. A rough guide to how much protein you should be eating is a gram for every two pounds of body weight. So if you weigh 160lbs you need to eat around 8g of protein per day.

You may see articles about nutrition refer to 'complete protein', which means it contains all the different amino acids your body needs but can't synthesise. Meat and animal products like eggs and dairy usually contain complete proteins, but you can also get what you need by eating a broad range of vegan protein sources like beans, chickpeas, quinoa, chia seeds, tofu and nuts. Stick to leaner meat like chicken and fish to avoid eating too much fat.

Fat

Fat is also a necessary part of a healthy diet, but most of us eat plenty of fat without trying. Unsaturated fats are best for you as they lower cholesterol instead of raising it, and you can get them from sources like nuts, avocados, eggs and yoghurt that are also healthy and full of vitamins and minerals.

Your body also burns fat for fuel, but it prefers glycogen because it's easier to burn. At all times you are burning both fat and carbohydrates, but at higher levels of intensity you will burn a higher proportion of carbs to fat because the energy they provide is more immediately accessible.

The problem is that in an endurance race like a marathon, it's impossible to eat enough carbohydrates to last you the whole way. At some point your body will have to switch to mostly burning fat, which contributes to the feeling that marathon runners call "hitting the wall", when breathing gets suddenly harder and your legs feel like lead.

Some nutritionists believe that eating a fairly low-carb diet while training or training after a short fast (such as in the mornings before breakfast) increases the level of enzymes associated with metabolising fat, allowing you to conserve your glycogen stores and run for longer without hitting the wall.

Micronutrients

A wide range of vitamins and minerals are necessary for your body for various structural and chemical functions. Eating a wide variety of fresh foods, and at least five portions of vegetables a day, will help you to get most of what you need.

Two of the most crucial nutrients for runners are calcium and iron. Running strengthens your bones as well as your muscles, but to do that you need adequate amounts of calcium. If you're not getting enough then you could be at increased risk of fractures and other skeletal injuries, and you have a higher chance of developing osteoporosis. You should be consuming 1000-1200mg of calcium every day, which is mostly found in dairy products.

Iron is one of the components of haemoglobin, which carries oxygen around the body. The efficient transport of oxygen to your muscles helps them work harder and recover faster. Iron is mainly found in meat and seafood, although dark leafy vegetables, beans, nuts and fortified cereal are also good sources. Women are more at risk of iron-deficiency than men because they lose blood every month during their periods; it's important to replace any lost iron or you will feel tired and short of breath.

While it's always best to get as many of your micronutrients as possible from your food, it can be very difficult to keep track of everything you're supposed to eat. There's no harm in also taking a multivitamin supplement as an insurance policy, and it will help fill in any short-term gaps in your diet.

Eating During Training

If you eat immediately before a run then you will feel heavy and uncomfortable with food bouncing around in your stomach. Eat at least 2-3 hours before a run, and then have a small snack like a flapjack or slice of toast around 30 minutes before you start.

During runs of more than an hour you will probably need to top-up your level of carbohydrates to keep your energy up. High GI options that are easily absorbed like sports drinks or energy gels work best.

Energy gels are very small and easy to eat on a run, and unlike solid food you won't be able to feel them rolling around in your stomach afterwards. Some runners prefer energy chews, which are more or less the same thing, or a carb-heavy sports drink.

Experiment with different things until you find something that keeps you going without upsetting your stomach. Whatever works for you on long training runs will also be the best strategy for race day.

When you've finished a run you need to feed your muscles with glycogen to stimulate them to repair themselves, and the maximal uptake of glycogen is in the first 30 minutes after your run.

Most people understandably don't feel like eating right after exercise, but replenishing your protein and carbohydrates with a yoghurt, cereal bar or sandwich will reduce muscle soreness the following day. Salty foods can help restore the salt lost during sweat, and will also stimulate your thirst so that you drink adequate amounts of fluid.

Eating on Race Day

Two to three days before your marathon you should start carb-loading; eating as much carbohydrate as possible. You need to build up the glycogen in your muscles and liver to fuel you for the race, and it needs a few days to accumulate. Rice, bread, porridge, pancakes, and pasta are ideal, and fruit is also good. Stay away from spicy food the day before the race, and eat foods you're used to rather than trying something new.

Don't be surprised if you've gained several pounds before the race. Carbohydrates make you retain water, which is a good thing in this case as you'll also be more hydrated for the race. Don't worry – you will lose it all after running 26 miles.

On the morning of the marathon have something plain that you would eat before a training session, like porridge or toast. Stay away from high-fat or high-protein foods, which will make you feel full and are harder to digest, but won't provide any easily-accessible energy. And don't eat too much fibre or you may have stomach troubles mid-race.

Water

The harder you work during your run, the hotter you get, and the more you sweat. Sweat is the primary way you lose water from your body during exercise (you also lose some by breathing), so the amount you're sweating is a good indicator of how much water you need. Hot days or long workouts call for more water than normal.

Running with a stomach full of water is as uncomfortable as a stomach full of food, so it's best to try to stay hydrated during the day rather than drink your daily requirement all at once. You need to drink around 2 to 3 litres of water per day, and try to avoid having too much caffeine or alcohol, since they have a dehydrating effect.

Slight dehydration during a run is normal and nothing to worry about; especially if you replenish your fluids once you're finished. Short runs (under an hour) only need water but if you've been out for longer than diluted juice or a sports drink will also replace much-needed sugar and sodium. During the race you should be drinking around 400-800 millilitres per hour, according to the International Marathon Medical Directors Association.

Be careful, though - it's entirely possible to drink too water and end up with low levels of sodium in your blood, or hypernatremia. This causes nausea and bloating, and in extreme cases can lead to seizures. Drinking when you're thirsty during a long run and then half a litre of water or a sports drink at the end should be enough to keep most people hydrated.

Sleep

During sleep your body repairs damaged tissue and builds up muscle and bone ready for you next workout. If you don't sleep enough and regularly then your body is unable to carry out the repairs it needs and you will feel worn down and under the weather. Your body responds to lack of sleep as stress and produces more cortisol, which also slows down recovery times.

The amount of sleep you need seems to vary from person to person. Some lucky people only need 5 hours a night to keep them healthy, but most of us need between seven and nine hours. Sticking to a regular sleep schedule, keeping the temperature in your bedroom cool and not having too much caffeine or alcohol will give you better quality sleep.

Exercises for Runners

There's more to keeping your body in great shape than just logging miles. You'll never even get to the start line of a marathon if you're injured, and better strength and flexibility combined with proper warm-up and cool down routines are the best way to keep injuries at bay. Strength and flexibility also mean faster times and better endurance, allowing you to finish your marathon with a personal best.

Warming Up

The purpose of a warm up is to elevate your heart rate and breathing, and raise your body temperature. This loosens your joints, speeds up your metabolic processes and increases the blood flow to the muscles to prepare them for your workout, reducing stiffness and risk of injury.

Start with some general mobility exercises for your whole body. Your movements should be slow and controlled and move through the full range of motion. Each one should be done five times:

- Bring your shoulders up towards your ears and roll them forward, then repeat the motion in the opposite direction.
- Stand with your feet hip-width apart and roll your hips in a circular motion.
- Stand with your feet hip-width apart, rotate your shoulders and upper torso to the left and then the right while keeping your hips facing forwards.

- Stand up straight and bring your left knee up to your chest, then lower to a standing position and switch legs.
- Bring your left foot up slowly behind you until level with your backside, then lower and switch sides.
- Hold one foot slightly off the floor and point your toes, then rotate the ankle in both directions. Switch feet.

A good pulse-raising activity before your run is walking. Start at a moderate pace for one minute and speed up for two minutes of fast walking before lightly jogging for two minutes.

For running-specific mobility exercises, do around 10-20 metres of the following at either walking pace or a light jog:

- **Walking lunge**: Take big steps forward, bending the knees over the toes and dropping your hips, until the knee of your back leg is close to the ground.
- **High knees**: lift each knee to hip height as you run, concentrating on the upward motion rather than travelling forwards, and keeping your back straight.
- **Back-kick**: as you walk or jog, extend your back swing and bring your heels up to touch your backside.
- **Crab**: Turn to the side and shuffle to your right for 10 metres, then spin the other way and shuffle to your left for 10 metres. Try to take long-ish strides and bring your feet together in between.
- **Skipping**: Skip forward on one foot, bringing your knee up as high as you can and using your arms for balance. Try to jump as high as possible on each foot.

Go back to a light jog and spend 3-5 minutes gradually building up your speed to your normal running pace. You are now warmed up and ready to start.

On the day of the marathon you don't want to do too much warming up or you will tire yourself out. A gentle ten-minute jog will get the blood flowing to the muscles and stimulate your nervous system. At the start line you won't have much room to move, and you may be in your corral for quite a while before the starting whistle, so a little jogging on the spot with high knees or dynamic lunges will keep you warm and not take up too much room.

Cooling Down

As blood is pumped around your body it carries oxygen and nutrients to the muscles, and takes away waste products like lactic acid. When you contract your muscles during exercise it helps push the blood back to the lungs to be re-oxygenated.

If you stop abruptly at the end of your run then your rapidly decreasing heart rate and relaxed muscles mean the blood and waste products remain in the muscles longer, which causes pain and swelling. A proper cool down will reduce how sore your muscles are the next day.

At the end of your run, slow down and incorporate 5 minutes of easy effort running, followed by 5 minutes of light jogging. Do the running-specific warm up exercises at gradually lower levels of intensity, and finish with 5 minutes of walking.

After a marathon, you can cool down on the finish line with ten minutes of walking, starting fast and gradually reducing your effort. Having a cold bath in the hour or so after running will reduce and swelling and combat the slight tearing of muscle fibres which leads to soreness the next day. Stretch your whole body a few hours after finishing, and get a massage the next day if you're very sore.

Stretching

Stretching is not the same thing as cooling down. The cool down allows your body to clear the lactic acid out of your muscles, while stretching makes you more flexible and lengthens the muscles and connective tissues around the joint to give you as much free movement as possible. This enhances performance and also contributes to preventing injury.

Exercise contracts your muscles, so stretching them out afterwards brings them back to their resting length. You should stretch your muscles while they're still warm, because the muscle fibres are more elastic, so just after your run when your body temperature is elevated is the perfect time. You can also stretch during your rest days, but warm up your muscles with a five minute walk or some other gentle movement first.

During static stretches, you want to hold each pose for 30 seconds before switching sides, and repeat each stretch twice. Keep your stretching steady and controlled; don't bounce during a stretch. Breathe in slowly and deeply and try to relax into the stretch, which can sometimes help you extend a little further. Never stretch to the point of pain.

Upper Body Stretches

- Stand with your feet hip-width apart. Hold your arms out in front of you and link your fingers, palms facing the body. Round your back and push forward through your shoulders and upper back.

- Link your fingers behind your back and gently pull your arms backwards, keeping them straight and your shoulders relaxed. You should feel the stretch across your chest.

- Hold your left arm across your body, so that your left hand is out to the right. Use your right hand to gently pull your upper left arm in towards your chest. You should feel it in your upper arm and shoulder. Switch sides.

- Extend your left arm above your head and then bend at the elbow so that your left hand is touching your neck or upper back. Use your right hand to gently pull your left elbow to the right, so that you can feel the stretch in your triceps. Switch sides.

Core Stretches

- Kneel on the floor on your hands and knees. Arch your back upwards and tilt your chin towards your chest, then lower your back and look up with your shoulders pulled back.

- Kneel down and sit back on your heels with your toes pointing behind you. Lean forward with your arms stretched out in front of you until your hands touch the floor, with your backside still touching your heels. You should feel the stretch in your lower back.

- Stand with your feet hip-distance apart and hands by your sides. Slide your left hand down the left side of your body and lean your torso down to the left, keeping your hips facing front. Repeat on the right.

Lower Body Stretches

- Standing up straight, pick up your left leg behind you until your heel is touching your backside, and hold your foot steady with your left hand. Your thighs should be aligned and your back straight, not arched. Switch legs.
- Take a big step forward with your right leg while keeping your left leg straight behind you. Push your left heel towards the ground and you should feel a stretch in your left calf as you lean forward. Keep your back and hips straight. Switch legs.
- Kneel on the floor and bring your left leg out in front of you, knee bent at a right angle. Push your right knee back slightly and, keeping your torso upright, push your hips forward until you can feel a stretch at the front of your hip. Hold for 30 seconds then switch sides.
- Sit upright on the floor with your legs crossed, and then widen your stance so the soles of your feet are touching. Gently press down on your knees to bring them closer to the floor, until you feel the stretch in your groin.
- Lie on your back with your knees bent and the bottom of your feet pressed against the wall. Bring your left ankle up in front of your right knee and hold it there. If you're close enough to the wall this should bring your lower back off the floor. As you breathe out, allow yourself to sink back down and you should feel the stretch in your left hip and glutes. Switch legs and repeat.

Strength Exercises

Some targeted strength training for your lower body will build up muscles that will help you run faster, keep going for longer and take steep hills in your stride. Stronger core muscles help you maintain your balance and good posture while running. Three sets of ten repetitions for each of these exercises, two to three times per week, will have you powering through your morning run in no time.

> **Plank**: kneel on the ground and lean forward to rest your weight on your elbows and forearms, then step your feet out behind you so you are in a press-up position but on your forearms instead of hands. Pull in your abdominals and hold for sixty seconds before lowering yourself to the ground.

> **Bridge**: lie on your back with your knees bent and feet flat on the floor. Keep your arms lying next to you or slightly out with your palms touching the floor for balance. Raise your hips off the floor and contract your glutes, keeping a straight line from shoulders to knees. Gradually lower your torso back to the ground.

> **Back Extensions**: lie face down on the floor with your arms and legs extended. Raise your head, left arm and right leg off the floor several inches, count to five, and then lower again. Repeat with the right arm and left leg.

Squat: stand upright with your feet hip-width apart. Bend your knees and sit back in your hips as though about to sit on an invisible chair. Go as low as you can comfortably manage, then slowly come back to the start position.

Lunge: take a deep step forward with your left foot and slowly lower your right knee until it is nearly touching the floor, keeping your torso straight. Switch legs.

Single Leg Squat: Holding on to the wall for balance if necessary, stand on one leg and bend the knee as far as you can comfortably go. Slowly push back up to starting position. After ten reps, turn so your other side is facing the wall and change legs.

Step Ups: stand in front of a step or low bench. Step up with the left foot and bring the right foot up next to it, then step down with the left foot and bring the right foot down. Then repeat with the right foot leading. Keep switching feet for 10 steps.

Calf Raises: Stand on a step with your heels hanging over the edge. Push up on to your toes, hold the position for a count of three, then slowly lower back down until your heel's below the edge of the step until you feel the stretch in your calf. Hold on to the wall for balance if necessary.

Mental Exercises

Making your body stronger and more flexible will help you run further, faster and with fewer injuries, but your mind plays almost as big a part as your body.

In 2009, researchers at Bangor University decided to test the effects of mental fatigue on performance. They gave one group of subjects a demanding cognitive task while a second group watched documentaries, and then asked them both to cycle to exhaustion.

Although their physiological response was the same – neither anaerobic threshold nor VO2 max were affected – the subjects who had done the demanding mental task reported higher levels of perceived exertion, and reached their point of exhaustion sooner than the control group.

What this means is that how tired you feel is not necessarily related to physical fatigue, but to how you feel mentally. A rough day at work, something worrying you, or just general low mood can all make you feel more tired than you really are. Pushing yourself through these times is a necessary part of running long distances, and completing your marathon training.

Forming the habit of running is the first and easiest way to get yourself out of the door even on bad days or horrible weather. Run on the same days at the same time if at all possible – you can experiment a bit during the first few weeks but once you find a time that suits you, stick to it.

If running is just the thing you do every other day after work, or first thing in the morning, or in the evening, then you will find yourself automatically lacing up your running shoes without having to put any thought into it.

Visualising your run might feel a bit silly, but it really does make a difference. If you tell yourself that you feel strong and energetic and visualise yourself running easily, you will have a more enjoyable run than if you imagine yourself exhausted and suffering.

Even if you *are* having a hard run, if you tell yourself you've got another mile in you then you will do it, and if you tell yourself that it's impossible and you can't then you will stop. There are limits to this technique, of course, but how you think of your run will have a big impact on your experience.

Positive thinking is another thing that feels a bit pointless to start with but makes a real difference to how you run. Tell yourself it doesn't matter if the weather is bad. Tell yourself you don't mind if you're tired. Tell yourself you love to run uphill.

Even though running can be tough sometimes, exercise also releases endorphins that make you feel good. You know the 'rush' you get when you're having a great run? If you focus on the positive parts and put the negative parts out of your mind you will be more motivated.

Most people think that motivation leads to action, but action can also increase your motivation. If you don't feel like doing that extra mile but you push yourself anyway, the feeling of triumph when you manage it will be something you remember next time you feel the same way, and you'll find it easier to push yourself again.

When you succeed at something you feel more motivated to pursue it, and when you're motivated you succeed even more, so force yourself to do better than you thought you could and it catapults you into a virtuous circle of desire and achievement.

By pushing yourself, however, we mean tell yourself you *can* do it, not that you *must* do it. Putting too much pressure on yourself makes any activity unpleasant instead of fun, and if running seems like a chore you have to do instead of a thing you love that will kill your motivation.

Endurance activities are best done in a fairly relaxed state. A sprinter might be able to charge themselves up to run 100 metres, but you can't maintain that state of excitement and energy over 26.2 miles. Instead loosen up your muscles if you're hunching, breathe deeply, and enjoy the experience of running.

Preparing to Run

Everybody runs slightly differently, and you should primarily run in a way that feels comfortable for you.

Having said that, a more efficient running style will make you better over longer distances, and is necessary to take on the endurance challenge of a marathon. Try to be mindful of your form and the way your feet strike the ground as you run, and adjust anything that's not quite working for you.

Correct Form

You should be looking ahead as much as possible rather than down at the ground (unless you're running over rough ground and need to watch your footing). Your head should stay fairly steady as you run; otherwise you're wasting energy propelling yourself up and down instead of forward. Some people have a tendency to hunch their shoulders as they run – if you find yourself doing this then take a breath and consciously relax your shoulders every five minutes until you get used to it.

If you're tired or pushing hard then it's tempting to lean forward for a little extra momentum, but you will breathe deeper and work better if you keep your shoulders back and torso upright. Gently pull in your abdominal muscles, but otherwise keep your upper body relaxed. Your arms should be bent at around 90 degrees at the elbow, and they should swing by your sides not across your body.

Keep your knees in line with your feet, and run so that your feet land underneath your knees and not too far in front of your body. You cannot push off from your toes properly if your feet are in front of your hips. Heavy heel striking can be a sign that your gait is too long.

Make sure that you're breathing properly – you should breathe through both the nose and the mouth to get the maximum amount of oxygen into your blood. Breathe from the diaphragm as much as possible, since the diaphragm muscle is stronger than the intercostal muscles between your ribs and will allow you to inhale more air. You know you're breathing from your diaphragm when your belly moves as much as your chest.

If you get a stitch in your side, the pain is caused by the diaphragm cramping, probably because of fatigue. Slow down and breathe slowly and deeply for a few minutes and it will go away. As you get fitter your diaphragm will get stronger and you should get far fewer side stitches.

Levels of Effort

You will need to expend different amounts of effort on different kinds of runs. Here's how the amount of effort you're putting in is commonly gauged:

- **Easy Pace/Conversational Pace**: At this level you can hold a conversation with someone without any problems. This is the pace used in warm ups or for the 'recovery' part of interval training (explained in the next section).
- **Moderate Pace**: you can talk in short sentences, but need to catch your breath in between. This is the right pace for steady runs.

- **Intense Pace**: you are breathing heavily and it is difficult to manage more than a few words at a time. This is the 'high effort' part of an interval run.

A more objective way to judge intensity is as a percentage of your maximal heart rate. A heart rate at 50-65% of your maximal heart rate would be an easy pace, 65-80% would be a moderate pace, and 80% to 90% would be an intense pace.

Working out your maximal heart rate requires you to wear a heart rate monitor while exercising at the absolute maximum effort you can manage for 5 minutes, which should be done under the supervision of a doctor or trainer.

You can also get your maximal heart rate by subtracting your age from 220, but this is a very rough estimate and not an absolute rule. If you don't have a heart monitor then the breathing comparisons above or your own assessment of the level of effort you're making will work just fine.

Different Types of Runs

There are a few different ways you can approach your runs, and a varied training program will improve all the different aspects of your running and make you marathon-ready in a way that simply running steadily can't accomplish.

Your speed during a run is a combination of your stride length and stride frequency. While being tall obviously helps your stride length, runners with long strides tend to have stronger leg and gluteal muscles and greater flexibility in their hips.

There's only so much you can do about your stride length, and most improvements in speed are down to stride frequency. Average runners manage around 100 steps per minute, elite long-distance runners between 180 and 200. Count how many steps you take in a minute and then try to gradually up the tempo, even if that means taking shorter steps.

- **Steady Paced Runs**: These will make up the bulk of your training. They improve your aerobic fitness and underpin all the other training that you do.
- **Interval Runs**: These runs alternate between fast bursts of effort and 'recovery' periods. When you start running your burst of effort might be a steady run and recovery period a fast walk, but as you progress your effort period should be an intense pace run and your recovery period should be an easy pace run. Interval runs are probably the best way of pushing up your speed and aerobic fitness.
- **Fartlek Runs**: These are similar to interval runs but less structured. Instead of alternating between two speeds for a fixed period of time, you run at a variety of different speeds using markers such as trees, buildings or fences to determine the length. This is more fun if you run with a partner because you can take it in turns to choose the speed and distance, and the unpredictability keeps you on your toes.
- **Hill Runs**: Uphill runs are great for building muscle strength and aerobic fitness, and help you develop your speed. Downhill runs strengthen the connective tissue and improve your stride rate. Aim for short, quick strides when running uphill. Introduce downhill running gradually with shallow slopes so you can control yourself.

- **Tempo Runs**: This is where you run at the 'lactate threshold', the speed above which you build up lactic acid in your muscles faster than your body can clear it away. Running at this threshold pushes it up, so that you can run steadily at a faster pace. It's not quite as fast as intense pace, meaning you can run for longer but still need slower breaks.
- **Endurance Runs**: These are long runs at an easy or moderate pace. They push your endurance and your ability to cover long miles without stopping up, and they should get progressively longer through your training. Don't worry about your speed during an endurance run; just concentrate on covering the miles.

Choosing a Route

Obviously, if you're going to include hill running in your training plan, you need to run a route that has hills on it. Depending on where you live this could be an impossible task or an inevitability, but try to plot out a route that has both gentle and harder inclines and plenty of flat to recover in between.

As you get closer to the marathon, the ideal running route is one that has a similar elevation profile to the race course. This is easier said than done, but at least check where the hills are in the course and try to make the hard and easy bits of your run somewhat similar. It will give you a feel for how tired you will be at different parts and how much strength you need to conserve for them. For example, one of the toughest parts of the Boston Marathon is the 'Newton Hills' from 17.5 miles to 21 miles, a set of steep inclines just when you're starting to run out of steam. It has defeated many a poorly prepared runner.

The chances are your marathon will be run on the road, so you need to do at least some of your training on the road too. If you are training for a cross-country marathon then you will want to run on the same terrain as the race, especially if you need to get used to running on rough ground.

Grass is an ideal surface to run on if it's smooth and the grass is short, because it absorbs some of the impact on your joints that hard surfaces deliver. It's harder to run on because the slight give means your muscles work harder to push you forward, but if you train on grass then running on the road will seem fast and easy in comparison.

Soft earth trails and sand are similarly good for building strength and lowering the risk of joint damage. Be aware, though, that soft surfaces can exacerbate injuries like Achilles tendonitis because your heel sinks too far back and strains the tendon. Uneven surfaces can also be dangerous because of the risk of tripping or twisting your ankle in a dip, and wet sand and mud are very slippery.

The road is inevitably where most of us run. They have street lights, handy if you're running at night or during dark winter days. Look for a route that has the minimum possible amount of traffic, and as few people as possible; quiet suburban streets are often the easiest to run in. Parks, waterfronts, and towpaths are good places if you're near the city centre.

Athletic tracks are also a good option if you can't find any quiet roads. They are guaranteed to be well lit and free from traffic, and the surface is completely even and reasonably gentle. If they're well maintained, then they may also be the only good outdoor option during icy or snowy weather.

The only drawbacks are that doing laps around them is pretty boring, and constantly curving in the same direction at either end of a loop can put stress on your knees and ankles.

Treadmills might seem appealing when it's cold and dark and you don't want to force yourself outside, but they're not a perfect substitute for real running. A 1% incline on a treadmill can mimic the extra effort outdoors from wind resistance and propelling yourself forward (as opposed to running on the spot), but it's harder to simulate running up and down hills or over uneven ground.

It's harder to do hill runs or interval training on a treadmill, and pretty much impossible to do fartlek sessions. Use a treadmill to maintain your fitness in the winter if you need to, but try to do most of your training outdoors.

If you choose a route that's not very familiar, then walk it once before you start as a test. Knowing if there are any obstacles ahead of you and which way you're going means you will be able to concentrate on your training program and timing your run without any distractions.

The Training Programme

We strongly advise that you consult your doctor before you start any training plan. You need to check your overall fitness level and ensure that you have no underlying conditions which could be exacerbated by training. Even if you're fit and healthy, having the numbers for things like blood pressure and cholesterol will give you a baseline for comparison to see how running is improving your health.

A doctor's visit is not only advisable but necessary if you:

- Are over 50 and don't already exercise regularly.
- Have a history of cardiac problems in your family.
- Have high blood pressure or cholesterol.
- Are more than 20 pounds' overweight.

Even if you've never done any running, you should still have a baseline level of moderate fitness before starting the programme, and be able to walk three miles in around an hour. If you struggle with that then pay your doctor a visit and start with some low to medium intensity walking until you can manage a mile in under 20 minutes.

The training plan covers a period of 26 weeks, or six months. That does not necessarily mean you will be able to complete a marathon in six months. Illness, injury, or other unforeseen circumstances can mean you need to rest and then repeat a week, and don't feel bad if you're tired or struggling and just need to stick at the same level for a few weeks.

It's important to go at your own pace and listen to your body, because if you push yourself too hard you risk injury. If you are already a runner, then skip forward to a week roughly equivalent to your current work out and start there.

There are three runs per week in the first few weeks, and then four runs per week as your fitness improves. Feel free to arrange your run days and rest days around your schedule. The only rule is that you should spread out your rest days over the week to give your body time to recover.

Have a rest day before and after your longest run and then take the other rest day between shorter runs. So, a sample run from week 12 might look like:

Monday	Tuesday	Wednesday	Thursday	Friday	Saturday	Sunday
Rest day	3 mile run with 5x 200m hill repeats	5 mile steady run	Rest day	3 mile Fartlek session	Rest day	8 mile endurance run

Or if you want to do your long run on Saturday and have Sunday off it might look like:

Monday	Tuesday	Wednesday	Thursday	Friday	Saturday	Sunday
3 mile run with 5x 200m hill repeats	Rest day	5 mile steady run	3 mile Fartlek session	Rest day	8 mile endurance run	Rest day

Running on the same days every week will make it easier to stick to your schedule.

Strength exercises, if you choose to do them, can be done on two of your rest days, after a short warm up, but do try to give yourself one complete day off every week. It's a good idea to stretch every day, either after running or after a short walk to warm your muscles.

Don't forget to warm up and cool down before and after each session. For the beginner program, you can do the general mobility exercises and a 5-minute walk to warm up and cool down, but once you reach the intermediate plan you want to do the whole warm up and cool down including running-specific mobility exercises.

Beginner			
	Session 1	*Session 2*	*Session 3*
Week 1	Run for 2 minutes Walk for 2 minutes Repeat x5	Run for 2 minutes Walk for 2 minutes Repeat x5	Run for 3 minutes Walk for 2 minutes Repeat x4
Week 2	Run 3 minutes Walk 2 minutes. Repeat x4	Run for 3 minutes Walk for 2 minutes Run for 4 minutes Walk for 2 minutes Run for 4 minutes Walk for 2 minutes Run for 3 minutes	Run for 3 minutes Walk for 2 minutes Run for 4 minutes Walk for 2 minutes Run for 4 minutes Walk for 2 minutes Run for 3 minutes
Week 3	Run for 3 minutes Walk for 1 minute Run for 5 minutes Walk for 2 minutes Run for 5 minutes Walk for 1 minute Run for 3 minutes	Run for 3 minutes Walk for 1 minute Run for 5 minutes Walk for 2 minutes Run for 5 minutes Walk for 1 minute Run for 3 minutes	Run for 4 minutes Walk for 1 minutes Run for 5 minutes Walk for 1 minute Run for 5 minutes Walk for 1 minute Run for 4 minutes
Week 4	Run for 4 minutes Walk for 1 minute Run for 5 minutes Walk for 1 minute Run for 5 minutes Walk for 1 minute Run for 4 minutes	Run 5 minutes Walk 1 minute Run 6 minutes Walk 1 minute Run 6 minutes Walk 1 minute Run 5 minutes	Run 5 minutes Walk 1 minute Run 6 minutes Walk 1 minutes Run 6 minutes Walk 1 minute Run 5 minutes
Week 5	Run 8 minutes Walk 2 minutes Run 8 minutes	Run 8 minutes Walk 2 minutes Run 8 minutes	Run 10 minutes Walk 2 minutes Run 10 minutes
Week 6	Run 10 minutes Walk 2 minutes Run 10 minutes	Run 15 minutes Walk 2 minutes Run 15 minutes	Run 15 minutes Walk 2 minutes Run 15 minutes
Week 7	Run 20 minutes Walk 2 minutes Run 10 minutes	Run 20 minutes Walk 2 minutes Run 10 minutes	Run for 25 minutes.
Week 8	Run for 25 minutes.	Run for 30 minutes.	Run for 30 minutes.

Intermediate

	Session 1	Session 2	Session 3	Session 4
Week 9	3 mile steady run	4 mile steady run	3 mile steady run	5 mile steady run
Week 10	3 mile steady run	4 mile steady run	3 mile steady run	6 mile steady run
Week 11	3 mile run with 5x 200m hill repeats (run up the hill then jog back down)	4 mile steady run	3 mile run including intervals: 60 seconds intense pace followed by 60 seconds easy pace x8	7 mile steady run
Week 12	3 mile run with 5x 200m hill repeats	5 mile steady run	3 mile Fartlek session	8 mile steady run
Week 13	3 mile run with 5x 200m hill repeats	5 mile steady run	3 mile run including intervals: 60 seconds intense pace followed by 60 seconds easy pace x8	10 mile endurance run
Week 14	4 mile steady run	5 mile steady run	4 mile steady run	12 mile endurance run
Week 15	4 mile run with 6x 200m hill repeats	6 mile steady run	4 mile run including intervals: 60 seconds intense pace followed by 60 seconds easy pace x10	12 mile endurance run
Week 16	4 mile run with 6x 200m hill repeats	6 mile steady run	4 mile Fartlek session	14 mile endurance run
Week 17	4 mile run with 6x 200m hill repeats	7 mile steady run	4 mile run including intervals: 60 seconds intense pace followed by 60 seconds easy pace x10	14 mile endurance run

Advanced

	Session 1	Session 2	Session 3	Session 4
Week 18	4 mile run with 6x 200m hill repeats	7 mile steady run	4 mile Fartlek session	16 mile endurance run
Week 19	5 mile steady run	8 mile steady run	5 mile steady run	16 mile endurance run
Week 20	5 mile tempo run: 5 mins at tempo pace alternated with 2 mins easy pace	8 mile steady run	5 mile run including intervals: 90 seconds intense pace followed by 90 seconds easy pace x7	18 mile endurance run
Week 21	5 mile run with 8x 200m hill repeats	8 mile steady run	5 mile Fartlek session	18 mile endurance run
Week 22	5 mile tempo run: 5 mins at tempo pace alternated with 2 mins easy pace	9 mile steady run	5 mile run including intervals: 90 seconds intense pace followed by 90 seconds easy pace x7	20 mile endurance run
Week 23	5 mile run with 8x 200m hill repeats	9 mile steady run	5 mile Fartlek session	20 mile endurance run
Week 24	4 mile steady run	6 mile steady run	4 mile steady run	12 mile steady run
Week 25	3 mile steady run	5 mile steady run	3 mile steady run	5 mile steady run
Week 26	3 mile steady run	3 mile walk	Rest day	Race Day! GOOD LUCK!

The reason the last three weeks are lighter is because you need to taper before a big race to rest. Your aerobic capacity won't suffer for a few easy weeks, and your muscles will get a chance to repair any minor damage and replenish their glycogen stores.

In the final week, it's not really necessary to run at all and it certainly won't make you more prepared at that late stage, but it can make you feel better to shake out your legs a bit and calm the nerves. You should keep stretching regardless of whether you're running or not.

From week 18 to week 23 you should start practising your fuel and fluid intake on your long runs, so that you know what you're going to do on marathon day. Try taking a gel every hour or so to avoid hitting the wall, and experiment with different flavours and brands to find one that works well. Try different amounts of water or sports drink and don't forget to drink steadily instead of downing it all at once.

Preventing and Dealing with Injury

The majority of running injuries are caused by overuse from pushing yourself and doing too much, too soon, too fast. Your distance and pace should build up steadily as you train so that you condition your muscular and skeletal systems. Always know your own limits, and don't do something if it's giving you pain. Remember, you're doing this for fun!

Weak muscles also cause injury, especially imbalanced ones. If some of your muscles have developed more than others, then your body won't be properly aligned as you run and you will be putting stress on the weakest parts. This can lead to – or be caused by – poor running technique or the wrong running shoes. Even the smallest change in your biomechanics makes a big difference over long miles, so double check your shoes and running technique.

The best way to treat most injuries is with the RICE method – rest, ice, compression, and elevation. Promptly ice any injury as soon as you get home to minimise swelling, and continue to ice it for 10-15 minutes three times a day for the next three days. Wrap a thin towel around the ice, don't apply it directly to your skin. If the swelling goes down then you can apply heat to the area if it relieves the pain, again with a towel wrapped around.

Compressing the area with an elasticated bandage for the next 48 hours and elevating it above chest level will also reduce the swelling, but be careful not to restrict the blood flow too much. If there is any tingling, numbness or pain then remove the compression bandage and just rest the injury. Non-steroidal anti-inflammatory drugs (NSAIDs) like aspirin or ibuprofen will also reduce swelling and relieve the pain.

Properly resting while injured is the most important thing you can do, but also the one most runners find the hardest – you worry about losing fitness and putting your training back, and not being prepared for the marathon. But if you do too much too soon you will be injured again, and that's more likely to put you out of the race than a little time off.

You can maintain your fitness while injured by cross-training, doing exercises that don't strain your injury. Swimming is one of the most low-impact exercises and works a wide range of muscle groups. Running in the pool is also great because it is low impact but higher resistance, meaning you build muscle while giving your injury time to heal.

It's usually still safe to cycle if you have shin splints or Achilles tendonitis, since cycling doesn't strain the same areas as running. Likewise, a session on the elliptical is fine for iliotibial band syndrome and runner's knee, and may also be okay if you have plantar fasciitis as long as you're not in pain while working out.

The elliptical is an especially good way to cross-train because of the similarity to running. Something gentle like yoga can also help but be careful you're not over-stretching and straining your injury.

Below are some of the most common injuries that affect long-distance runners.

Runner's Knee

What is it? - Sometimes known as Patellofemoral Pain Syndrome, this is one of the most common running injuries.

Symptoms - Vague pain around the knee or pain focused behind the kneecap, discomfort while sitting with knees bent.

Causes - A substantial increase in running miles or intensity of training; misalignment of the patella in the femoral groove.

Treatment - Rest and ice are recommended, and NSAIDs will help reduce pain and swelling. Stretches and exercises that strengthen the quadriceps will help the knee track correctly and reduce the chances of it recurring.

Iliotibial Band Syndrome

What is it? - The iliotibial band is a ligament that runs from your hip down the outside of your leg. Continuous movement as it rubs against the bottom of your femur can cause it to become inflamed.

Symptoms – Pain just above the knee joint, especially when the foot strikes the ground, and swelling of the tissue on the outside of the knee.

Causes – Running too many miles, or anything that turns the knee inward often like running downhill or on a banked surface.

Treatment – The usual rest, ice and compression will usually sort this out, or in more severe cases massage, ultrasound and cortisone injections may help the healing process.

Patellar Tendonitis

What is it? - Inflammation of the tendons around the kneecap.

Symptoms – Pain at the front of the knee, red and swollen knees, and warmth around the knee joint.

Causes – This is sometimes called 'jumper's knee' because it is common in activities that involve a lot of jumping. If you play basketball or volleyball as well as running, then they might put you at further risk.

Treatment – Rest, ice and compression are usually recommended, and immobilising your knee can prevent you from further aggravating it. Physical therapy might be necessary in severe cases.

Shin Splints

What is it? - Also known as Medial Tibia Stress Syndrome, these are thought to be related to inflammation of the connective tissue or a stress reaction.

Symptoms – Pain down the front of your lower legs during exercise, which fades or goes away when resting.
Causes – Weight bearing activities on the legs; being overweight, suddenly starting a longer and harder training plan, or running on very hard surfaces can all contribute.

Treatment – These are not a serious injury and rest; ice and painkillers will cure you. Do some low impact exercise like swimming or yoga to keep fit while you heal.

Stress Fractures

What is it? - If you don't rest after you get shin splints then this is the next step; tiny cracks in the bone caused by cumulative stress rather than a single impact.

Symptoms – Pain in the front lower legs, heel, or foot during standing, walking or running, in a more localised area than shin splints.

Causes – Overuse. If you've been pushing yourself too hard and doing too much high-impact exercise, then you will end up with a fracture.

Treatment – You need to completely stop running, probably for one to three. Visit your doctor, as in some cases crutches or a plaster cast are necessary.

Achilles Tendonitis

What is it? - The inflammation of the Achilles tendon, which connects the calf muscles and heel at the back of the leg.

Symptoms - Pain along the back of your foot and above the heel, stiffness in the mornings and after sitting for long periods.

Causes - Anything that strains your calves, like hills or speed work. Over pronating when running, or shoes with two much cushioning that allow your heel to sink too far and strain the tendon.

Treatment – Stop running or cut back as soon as you start to feel it. Even if the pain is only slight, running through it will make it worse and bad cases can last for months. Elevation, icing and NSAIDs will all help but avoid too much compression, which restricts the blood flow to the tendon and slows down recovery. Calf raises will strengthen the tendon.

Plantar Fasciitis

What is it? - Small tears and inflammation in the ligaments on the underside of the foot.

Symptoms – Pain in the heel and bottom of the foot, especially first thing in the morning.

Causes – Repetitive microtrauma (caused by running harder or longer than usual); low arches and overpronation; and standing for long periods of time, especially on hard surfaces.

Treatment – Rest, ice and NSAIDs; extra cushioning in your shoes, particularly around the heel; gentle stretching of the foot and calf.

Pulled Muscle

What is it? - Tears in the muscle fibres and possibly the tendon, sometimes with damage to small blood vessels and localised bleeding.

Symptoms – Swelling and bruising in the muscle, pain when using the muscle and when resting, stiffness.

Causes – Putting an abnormal amount of pressure on the muscles during activities or sports.

Treatment – Rest, ice, elevation and NSAIDs – sound familiar? If you have a significant injury, a fever, or don't feel any better after 48 hours then consult your doctor.

The Big Day

How to Choose a Marathon

A lot of new marathon runners are surprised by how difficult the big marathons are to get into, and how far in advance you need to prepare.

For example, the London Marathon uses a ballot to determine who gets a place, as do many of the other big races, and for the 2017 marathon there were 253,930 applicants for 50,000 places. And you need to plan in advance, because ballots are open for five days in May for the race the following April. The bigger a marathon is the higher the entry fees usually are, which you may also want to take into consideration.

If you're entering a marathon as part of a running club, the club should take care of your entrance application. There are often a certain number of places allocated to club runners, and the rules for entry may be different. If you're running on behalf of a charity then you should apply through the charity, as again there will be a certain number of allocated places. Many charities have a minimum amount of sponsorship money they expect you to raise before you can race for them.

For your first marathon, it's safest to stick to something close to home. Training in the same terrain and weather and being familiar with them both will make things easier on you, and not having to worry about travelling, booking accommodation or unfamiliar food and routines will allow you to concentrate completely on your running.

Don't choose a marathon that takes place in the toughest weather for you – if you hate the heat then avoid races in the middle of summer, and if you struggle more in the cold then don't enter a race in the depths of winter.

Not surprisingly, spring and autumn races are the most popular. If you're a morning or evening runner and most comfortable with that then you will probably find it easier if you choose a marathon that has a similar time. Dragging yourself out of bed for a run when you're not used to it won't do your race time any good.

Week of the Race

As has already been mentioned, your training should taper off in the two to three weeks before a race to give your body time to rest. Eat plenty of carbohydrates and drink water to fill up your muscles with glycogen and hydrate yourself in the days before the race.

Rest completely two days before the race and then take a short run – an easy two or three miles – the day before the race. This prevents that feeling of stiffness and unfamiliarity that can plague you at the start of the race if you haven't run for a few days.

The week before the race is not the time to try anything new. Stick to your usual routine, go to bed at the same time, eat the same things, wear the same clothes to race that you wear to train. If you're racing in lighter performance shoes instead of your usual trainers then do a couple of runs during training and a short one the week of the race to make sure there are no problems.

It's common to suffer from last-minute nerves and start doubting yourself – have I done enough? Can I sneak in another run? Don't start doubting yourself now. Take a look at your training log, review everything you've done, and trust in your own preparation.

If you've never been to the marathon location before then check out the route on a map and work out how long it will take you to get there – then add on some time for bad traffic or other disasters. Find out where you can park near the race and have a back-up plan if it's full. Big races almost never have enough parking, so consider public transport if that's a viable option for you.

Check out the map of the race course and make a note of where the water stations are and where the toilets are located. Even if you sweat out most of the water you may still need to use them, and the running motion can sometimes have an effect on your bowels – part of the reason you shouldn't eat too much in the morning and stick to familiar foods.

Lay out your shoes and clothes the night before the race and double-check you haven't forgotten anything. You will probably need:

- Race number (unless you're collecting it in the morning)
- Timing chip (which officials uses to time your race)
- Running watch
- Sunscreen
- Sunglasses
- Water bottle (if you want your own)

- Sports gels or snacks
- Plasters
- Something to wear after the race –
  a jacket/hoodie/compression gear
- Towel

Race Day

You will probably be awake early on race day, as the nerves kick in and you mentally prepare yourself for what's to come. Eat a small carbohydrate-heavy meal at least two hours before the race so you have time to digest it. A couple of slices of toast or a bowl of cereal are ideal, but above all stick to something familiar. And drink a large glass of water to make sure you're completely hydrated.

Another couple of things you can do to increase your comfort during the race are to trim your toenails short and rounded so you don't bruise your toes, and put some Vaseline or plasters over your nipples (if you're a man) so the shirt you're wearing doesn't chafe as you run.

Make sure you leave yourself plenty of time to get to the race, since there may be thousands of other people also heading in the same direction. Pick up your race number if it wasn't sent out in advance and anything else you need from the officials. There will be a lot of people milling around at the start, and possibly stalls advertising running gear, but try not to get distracted by the noise and crowds. Focus your mind on the race.

You may be hanging around at the start line for a couple of hours if you're part of a big race. Depending on the weather you may be cold while waiting but warm up quickly as soon as you start to run, which means you're going to need warm clothes to start and then cooler ones.

Lots of runners bring an old sweater and trousers that they can discard at the start of the race or at the first station. You can wrap your sweater around your waist when you get hot but you will probably find this uncomfortable over the long miles.

If it's raining you may very well see people wearing bin bags to keep the rain off, which they can then throw away once they get started. Spare gear can also be put in your kit bag, which will be transported to the finish line where you can pick it up.

You want to do the minimum amount of warm-up necessary, so that you don't use up too much of your glycogen reserves. If you're not aiming for a very fast time, you can take the first mile slowly while you warm up cold muscles. If you're planning to hit targets for each mile, warm up at the start with a short 10-minute jog and then some gentle stretching. Time your warm-up so that you're finishing it just as you get herded into place at the start line.

During the Race

Pace yourself. Start off too fast and you'll be exhausted before you're half way through. Excitement and nerves will probably make you run faster than usual at the start, so check your watch against the mile markers and check you're not out-running yourself.

Big races often have pacemakers; experienced runners who help newcomers pace the distances for a specific goal time. They run at a steady speed, so if you know you're aiming for a certain time then running with them, or at least keeping an eye on them, will tell you if you're going too fast or slow.

Don't wait until you hit the wall to take an energy gel or bar. Your body needs time to digest and process the fuel before it reaches your muscles, so you want to be taking in carbohydrates evenly and consistently so that you never hit the wall in the first place.

Take something in the first five miles, even though you won't feel like you need it, to restock your glycogen stores. If you're not sure how much to eat, around 60g of carbohydrates per hour should be enough to keep you going without making you feel heavy.

Although you do need to hydrate, it's normal to be a bit dehydrated during a race and, as mentioned in the Nutrition section, it is possible to drink too much water and lower the levels of salt in your blood.

Try to drink at least 400 millilitres in the first hour so you don't end up drinking too much later and running with a stomach full of water sloshing around inside you. Other than that minimum, let your thirst be your guide. The amount of water you can comfortably drink during training will give you an idea of how much you should be drinking now.

After you cross the finish line, walk around for a bit to cool down and drink some more water. Try to eat a small snack even if you don't have an appetite. You will want to go and pick up your medal or certificate if the marathon provides one, and get confirmation of your time.

Make sure to get enough sleep the night after the race, as it will help your body recover better, and give it at least five days before you start running again. The high of completing your first marathon will have you enthusiastic to start training for the next, but you need to let your body rest a bit first.

Above all, enjoy yourself during the race, and congratulate yourself afterwards on a job well done. Go out to celebrate with friends and family, or at least reward yourself with anything you haven't been allowed to eat or drink during your training. Don't dwell on anything that went wrong or wonder if you could have run a better time, but remind yourself that you've just achieved something extraordinary.

What Now?

Congratulations! You just ran a marathon, and you should be very proud. And if you feel the urge to display your medal on the mantelpiece and tell the story to your family and friends for the umpteenth time, go for it – you've earned it!

Don't be surprised if you're sore in the days after the marathon, and swear that you'll never run another. Don't worry – marathon running is addictive. Having completed one, may find yourself starting to set your sights higher; a faster time, a tougher race, a different terrain, an exotic location.

If you want to set a personal best in the next one then keep working on your interval training and hill runs, and keep trying to push up your strides per minute. Increase your weekly mileage by a little at a time and you will get even fitter and faster, and be in even better shape to tackle the next one.

If you're looking for a really big challenge then ultra-marathons are even longer races, often multi-day events with challenging hills or weather conditions and a group of truly dedicated runners undertaking them.

For example, the Sundown Marathon in Singapore is twice the length of a marathon and run through the city at night, while the Marathon des Sables, widely considered to be the toughest foot race on Earth, is run through the Sahara over the course of six days. Marathons can open up all kinds of incredible experiences.

Even if you're not training for another marathon, keep running. The health benefits are enormous; stronger muscles, more energy, resistance to disease. Running helps prevent obesity, type 2 diabetes, high blood pressure, strokes and heart disease, and reduces the risk of some cancers, and it can add years to your lifespan.

It's also an ideal opportunity to get away from everybody else for a while and clear your mind, and exercise boosts your endorphins and improves your mood. Lots of runners say they depend on their runs for their mental as well as physical health.

Running a marathon takes dedication, persistence and self-discipline, qualities that are beneficial in every area of life. Having achieved this, there's nothing stopping you from applying the lessons you've learned here to any other goal you might have. You can do anything you set your mind to.

Made in the USA
Las Vegas, NV
01 June 2023

72822040R00039